SEASON'S BELLE

A Labrador Retriever's First Year

By Bob Butz

Photographs by Lee Thomas Kjos

CAMDEN, MAINE

In slightly different form, portions of this book have appeared in *The Retriever Journal, The Pointing Dog Journal, Traverse: Northern Michigan's Magazine,* and *Shooting Sportsman.*

Dust jacket and interior design by Phil Schirmer

Printed in China

7   6   5   4   3   2   1

ISBN 0-89272-507-9

Library of Congress Control Number: 2002104987

COUNTRYSPORT PRESS

Camden, Maine

For catalog information and book orders, call 800-685-7962,
or visit www.downeastbooks.com

DEDICATION

For Nancy

ACKNOWLEDGMENTS

Like so many great Labrador retrievers, Belle came into this world under the watchful eye of Mary Howley of Candlewood Kennel. And, of course, I'm grateful to Rick Finger and his family, who cared for Belle in the first seven weeks before placing her on a jet plane for the hop over Lake Michigan to me. Thanks to Pam Johnson, The Canine Coach of Traverse City, a great trainer who treats every dog under her charge as if it was her own. I appreciate, too, Dr. David Burke, Dr. Jerry Harrison, and the staff of the Grand Traverse Veterinary Hospital. My thanks also go to Steve Smith, Don Thomas, and my good friends John Shoemaker, Doug and Anne Stanton, and Greg and Dianne Nicolaou for their personal and professional support.

One of the greatest things to come of this book, outside of a wonderful hunting dog, is my relationship with editor Chris Cornell and, especially, with photographer Lee Thomas Kjos. Without the dedication both showed to the project, this book would not have been possible.

PARTNERS

Like children, puppies start out belonging only to us. We feed them, dote on them, and hold them close. And in return they fast become ours in a singular, uncompromising way.

The relationship evolves slowly. At first we are hardly more than mere littermates in their eyes. But as we lead them through tangles of spring grass and freshets of cold melt water, a kind of stewardship develops, and we become a teacher, one whose responsibility it is to channel the pup's boundless energy and desire.

The blood of some dogs destines them to be hunters. And for them, once the turnabout from puppy to dog is complete, we find that they are never wholly ours again. The good ones become our partners, commanded less by us than by this thing we call instinct—a witch's brew of wind and scent that triggers something way back in the recesses of the canine mind.

The Spanish philosopher Jose Ortega y Gasset, author of the book *Meditations on Hunting*, called that arrangement in the field between hunter and dog a "collaboration." But there's more to this partnership, as any dog man would unabashedly admit. Truth is, most friendships—and even some family ties—aren't half as strong.

At our age, my wife and I should have been thinking of babies not Labrador retriever puppies. But, in Nancy's defense, I'm mostly to blame.

Hunt behind a great bird dog, and you'll come to want one of your own.

The great ones cast that kind of magic over you.

I was lucky enough to own a really fine bird dog already. And if the old saw is true, you're only granted one in a lifetime. But I longed for another. Admittedly, I'm a fiend. I *needed* another dog. You see, the junkie in me craves few things more than that warm kick of adrenaline I get when following a dog hell-bent for leather on bird scent.

Harper was only into his fourth year, the leading edge of his prime. He has always had within him what D. H. Lawrence called "quickness," the "god's flame." So totally alive is his spirit, so hot is his blood—his instinct for finding and retrieving birds—that even my boorish, ham-handed attempts at training somehow didn't ruin him totally.

Friends who have hunted with us will attest to Harper's faults, which in the eyes of some may far outweigh his virtues. But no one could ever say he's not

a sheer wizard at finding birds.

In the field, he's a juggernaut—a balls-to-the-wall black devil dog. Among his faults, he's utterly headstrong and a veritable screamer in the duck blind when the birds start dropping in.

These howling fits are the worst. We're not talking about a little sissy whimpering. The noise at times is an all-out wailing, a caterwaul as if his insides are on a slow boil. For years I tried to break Harper of this. I did some unimaginable things to make him stop, things I'm embarrassed to admit now. But his intensity is too strong. So now I've come to just accept this as part of the deal. A friend once summed it up: "Harper has issues." But down a mallard, and you'll bear witness to a rooster tail of white froth in his wake.

Should I even mention that in four years of hunting

with Harper, he has never lost a bird?

Greatness, like beauty, is in the eye of the beholder. Which is the long way around saying that despite his eccentricities, Harper suits me just fine.

In fact, I've often daydreamed of owning a kennel full of Labradors just like him. Come autumn, I'd turn every one of them out into my grouse and woodcock covers—cast loose from the truck this veritable bird-hunting wrecking crew, stand back, and watch them running roughshod, the birds they routed up taking to the air in singles and pairs like fireballs from a Roman candle.

It's sheer gluttony that made me want another, a cretin's desire.

I wanted to run with a pack.

• • •

But I wanted a bit of balance, too. Harper's the offspring of field-trial parents—a dog bred to move and move fast, a hunter with no other urgings in life beyond finding birds and fetching. He was the alpha male of his litter, a pile of puppies with a better pedigree than my own.

I wanted the boldest one in the litter, because being a new trainer I was destined to make plenty of mistakes. Hard dogs bounce back better than soft ones from inept handling. But I would holler and cuss myself hoarse

A friend once summed it up: "Harper has issues." But down a mallard, and you'll bear witness to a rooster tail of white froth in his wake.

5

I went looking for a nice, sleepy female,

a gentle puppy that would like sitting in

my lap and being stroked under the chin.

I was granted just such a pup, a little

lady, under circumstances clearly divine.

Belle, you see, came from a litter of one.

with Harper during his early training, lie in bed at night pitying myself as hopelessly over-dogged.

When John Madson wrote, "It was hunting with all the fat rendered away, and reduced to the clean white bone," he was talking of late-season pheasants. But this also describes hunting behind Harper—or for that matter, your typical Labrador retriever.

Hunting with a Lab is about sore legs, mud, and sweat. After a few seasons behind a good Lab, you have a hard time keeping track of all the glorious flushes and amazing retrieves. With Harper it sometimes feels as if I'm trying to pinpoint a lightening strike or trying to catch a clap of thunder. So I went looking for another dog to complement him. The yin to his yang. A dog that might lend itself to the balance I sought.

Belle is the name of a beauty. Fitting, given that Harper's such a beast. And to that end—or beginning, depending on how you look at it—I went looking for a nice, sleepy female, a gentle puppy that would like sitting in my lap and being stroked under the chin. I was granted just such a pup, a little lady, under circumstances clearly divine.

Belle, you see, came from a litter of one.

"One puppy?"

Friends whom I told would say it just like that. Incredulous.

But always, again: "One puppy!" This time, agog.

Instead of trepidation, I felt giddy at the news. *One puppy!* And a yellow female at that. It was nothing less than a sign. The magic of it was too much to ignore. Being a mite superstitious, I needed only a short leap to convince myself that this little lady was sent specifically for me, that the fates had spoken, and that already our future together was preordained.

• • •

Exactly how Harper would get along with a new puppy was cause for concern. Not that he's unpredictable or vicious. A typical Labrador, Harper's a consummate lug and a bit of a pushover at times. Still, everybody can relate a story about the big, dopey, otherwise friendly older dog that resents the attention the new puppy gets, becomes cantankerous, grows reclusive, or suddenly goes nutso one day and sends the pup to the vet.

But the only thing that stands out about Belle's homecoming was how blithely Harper took the whole thing. It was actually a letdown for Nancy and me. One obligatory sniff and he retired to his bed and doggie dreamland, seemingly less miffed by the pup than by our rousting him from visions of greenheads cartwheeling to the water and white bumpers falling from the sky like snow.

He barely raised an eye when Belle sauntered over to him, took up a mouthful of his ear, and chomped down hard enough that Nancy and I both winced. The pup then went to his tail, momentarily transfixed by its cobralike sway. She took a good hold of that next. Harper yawned and rolled over on his back.

"Oh, that's so cute," Nancy said.

The scene had cast a spell. Belle pawed twice at Harper's undulating tail, a moment of puppyness both playful and innocent. But then she stepped back as if sizing up the problem and cocked her head quizzically at his underbelly.

In defense of what followed, Nancy would later say that Belle was merely trying to nurse. Yet, I think otherwise. The strike was too quick and most definitely directed at a spot never meant for biting.

Harper snarled and snapped. Every imaged horror flashed before me but was gone faster than it took Belle to yip and jump back. There was no need to admonish Harper and add insult to injury. As for Belle, she was undaunted. She ran a wild, loping circle around the living room—her stumpy, seemingly jointless legs carrying her in a kind of hobbyhorse gait. Then she stopped, squatted rather purposefully, and peed on the middle of the floor.

APRIL

Northern Michigan. Ours is a particularly snowy country, where a hundred and fifty inches of powder shower from the heavens half of the year. Up here, you can spend so much time dogged by winter that you begin cursing the season under your breath. Winters up here have personality, even if it is that of an uncouth dinner guest who arrives too early and stays too late.

I consider myself a winter person. But Belle's first year found me lusting for signs of spring. The season never kicks off precisely on the day the calendar says it

12

should. In fact, most of April allowed little satisfaction. No showers. No flowers. Gray skies and every day more snow blowing down from the north, over the big water.

As I had with Harper, I shoveled out a toilet space in the backyard and borrowed a phrase from one of my training books. "Hurry up. Hurry up." became the mantra for Belle doing her thing. Beyond these potty breaks and intervals of playtime throughout the day, Belle spent most of her time in the kennel. Accidents in the house were rare, and when they happened, simply catching her in the act and firmly chiding her was enough to bring on the most defeated, sad-eyed look she could muster.

Unlike Harper, who initially abhorred "the box," loathed it as if the crate were some canine-torture apparatus, Belle first took to crate training with complete indifference.

But her tolerance for it wasted away with the snow, which by month's end was lying in dirty piles, rotting in the shade. Belle's world grew larger by the day. The wind shifted from north to south, and with it came a warm breeze that smelled of mud and earth. Like cathedral light through stained glass, shafts of orange pierced the gray snow clouds and ran the guts of winter through.

Winter holds on so long here, you can forget what the world looks like without snow. You think you

She ran a wild, loping circle around the living room—her stumpy, seemingly jointless legs carrying her in a kind of hobbyhorse gait. Then she stopped, squatted rather purposefully, and peed on the middle of the floor.

13

To a puppy born in winter,

the smells that come up

from the ground must

simply overwhelm.

remember, but the memory is dull—and just how fuzzy the vision is becomes clear when you finally see bare earth again. Green grass! It tickles your insides, makes you giddy. Makes you smile.

To a puppy born in winter, the smells that come up from the ground must simply overwhelm. To my crippled senses, spring air is simply dank and fog-heavy, thick and sometimes hard to breathe. With the land and water and everything that crawls and swims so long frozen beneath the ice and snow, oxygen deprived, it's as if they are gasping for air all at once. Even with that feeling, which to me is distinctly spring, I was waiting for something more definitive.

Again, always looking for a sign.

After weeks of blessed silence and uninterrupted sleep, Belle became fed up with the kennel one night, waking on a half-dozen occasions, yipping and yowling to escape her confines. A sucker for the ruse, I rose every time.

But in the backyard, her business was fast forgotten. I stood there groggy, stiff-legged, and sore-backed while she snorkeled around my feet. More new smells. Night smells. Another dog barked as I tried hurrying the process along.

But it wasn't a dog I heard. It was geese, what were soon dozens—perhaps a hundred—honking to one

17

another in staggered lines just over the trees. They appeared as silhouettes in the night sky, moon shadows flecked by the stars. The hullabaloo was such that even Belle stopped with the sniffing and gazed skyward.

"Whatta ya think of that, Belle?" I asked when the sound of their passing died away. But she was already back nosing at the ground.

I turned the way the geese had flown, straining in the quiet to hear them and imagining for a moment that I could. I remembered what Aldo Leopold said, "One swallow does not make a summer, but one skein of geese, cleaving the murk of a March thaw, is the spring."

When I looked back at Belle, she was merrily gnawing on a pinecone, lost in a moment of her own.

MAY

When it comes to hunting I'm both a generalist and an opportunist, which is to say that my interests tend to skew. I like snowy, frostbit mornings in the duck blind as much as those warm-weather October romps through the grouse and woodcock covers. If we bumble into a pheasant or bust a covey of quail, so be it. I prefer a dog that can not only do it all, but can do it all well. This, of course, describes your typical Labrador retriever.

Labs suit me for other reasons. Because I am such a muddler, I require a dog that takes to the game instinctively. When it comes to training, a well-bred Lab is virtually "idiot proof," that is, the easiest of hunting dogs to train. For myself, I use the word "training" in the most elemental of sense, as my approach could probably be called lackadaisical.

Admittedly, I'm no sergeant-at-arms; I like to let my dogs be dogs. This I attribute, at least in part, to growing up on a farm where there was always a dog or two around. Except for Brownie, my father's feisty brown Chihuahua, there were never any purebreds in the lot. But every one of them hunted, even Brownie, who rode around in my father's hunting coat and was called into action any time there was a bird or rabbit holed up in a tangle and in need of a rout.

In my recollection, Daddy never formally trained a hunting dog in his life. Yet he seemed to enjoy quite a rapport with all of them. It was his belief that a dog learned best by doing and that by letting dogs be dogs, you'd learn far more from them than they'd ever learn from you. According to my father, a dog was supposed to be trained to the extent that it stayed within range and came when you called it.

Of course, I haven't totally kept with this philosophy. To learn the rudiments of retriever training, I've relied on books and dog-training videos. Surely, if you placed three dog trainers in a room the only thing

I remembered what Aldo Leopold said,

"One swallow does not make a summer,

but one skein of geese, cleaving the murk

of a March thaw, is the spring."

19

any two of them would agree on was that the third was doing something wrong. Somehow, though, I've managed to cut through the bull and cobble together an amateurish training regimen that works.

Ultimately, I'd rather live with my dogs than lord over them. I'd rather trust good breeding, and—in the tradition of my father—believe in the fates that a strong bond developed will result in some kind of partnership between us in the field.

• • •

A true desire to hunt and retrieve is something born into some dogs; it cannot be taught. But the desire in Lab puppies lacks focus, is unchanneled and unrefined. In the beginning it's a frantic, uncontrollable oral fixation they have, not only to carry but also to seek out, gnaw, and shred everything except the carload of chew toys you bought specifically for this purpose.

Belle chased after the tiny canvas puppy bumper I routinely tossed for her in the kitchen and returned without hesitation. She instinctively loved the game, though to keep her enthusiasm up I was careful to quit long before she grew weary of it.

Between time-outs in "the box,"

Ultimately, I'd rather live with my dogs than lord over them. . .a strong bond developed will result in some kind of partnership between us in the field.

. . . she occasionally fell into heavenly puppy sleep on the wood floor in the mudroom, snoring quite unladylike in the warm patch of sunlight there.

between blissful chewing fits, her feedings twice a day, and her chomping Harper's ears and neck into a sloppy, sodden scruff—a pastime that he actually seemed to enjoy—she occasionally fell into heavenly puppy sleep on the wood floor in the mudroom, snoring quite unladylike in the warm patch of sunlight there. It was the only time she was not underfoot, not studying my every move with her ebony eyes trusting as those of a fawn.

We played another game, this one to bolster her hunting instinct, which was more easily directed. We started with the paltry number of woodcock and grouse wings I had collected last season. Contrary to years past, I had had more luck connecting with incoming mallards and big cock pheasants slow on the rise. So my wing stash of the latter two species was considerable. Good thing, as Belle loved the game; we were into the reserves within a week.

I stashed the wings in various hiding places throughout the house and set Belle about the task of finding them. As she became more proficient, the searches became more and more difficult when I began laying down scent trails on the wife's Berber. And even though a thawed wing was hardly a tasteless plastic bumper, with a little encouragement she always returned to me with her find, chomping gleefully.

A falconer friend of mine had taught me a trick that he used every time his goshawk Fire came down with bird. In his pack, he always carried with him a baggie full of chicken heads. After those glorious chases when Fire came tumbling to the ground with her prize, Jack would calmly approach the mantling bird, come in behind her, and with slight of hand substitute the chicken head for the brains of the bird she had captured and was now feasting on.

Belle was easily duped in kind. For her, a Milk Bone was enough of a distraction, just the trick to scrabble

her little puppy mind. I was desperate to see what she'd do with a whole bird. But because I'm both a lousy shot and a glutton for the flavor of wildfowl, I had plucked all my birds for the table, saving none for fetching practice.

With my stash dwindling by the day and no open season showing on the calendar, I tried tying the remaining wings around canvas bumpers to teach Belle to seek out and retrieve items that had not only the smell of a bird but also the appropriate size and weight. Logical, yes?

But that Belle was proving to be a smart one. The first time I hid one of these stand-in birds, she found it behind the couch with little trouble. All I could see was her tail going in circles, her rear end wiggling. What I could *not* see was her teeth biting neatly through the tether that secured the wings to the "bird." She emerged bumperless. I was crestfallen. We obviously had some work to do.

And I needed to find us some birds.

S U M M E R

THE LEARNING TIME

Hunters and their dogs are, as the writer Rick Bass observed, farmers of a kind. Think of the gun as the hunter's scythe, the dog as a draft horse that pulls the plow. Come autumn, you both take to the fields together, cutting paths in the bird covers as distinct as blackened furrows etched in sod by the plow.

You might remember, however, when this partnership was young—the hot summer months, the learning time, long before the dog came to know the bird covers and to understand the work better than you. This is when we hunters cultivated seeds of a different kind.

Gingerly we tended to those green shoots of drive and desire. We tried hard to instill confidence, of which there was never enough. Confidence in a gun dog is like rain. And like a bolt of lightening and a clap of thunder, the day a puppy bounds over the training field in front of us and leaps into the air on the tail of a rising bird, it's certain to rattle the glass of a hunter's soul. For when those four feet touch the ground, we have in our charge a gun dog.

But it's summer now, and our young partner has not yet proven herself. So again like a farmer we stare into the western sky, praying for a cloudburst. And when it comes, we will cup our hands to the heavens and try to catch hold of it. Yet these things come from beyond, seemingly from nowhere, and always slip through our fingers like rain.

JUNE

This has been a month of firsts, a month of changes. Every day a certain part of Belle's anatomy grows a little, yet nothing in proportion to anything else. Nothing seems to fit. Her tail is too long one day; her head is too big the next. Every appendage keeps losing pace with her thickening legs and hugely padded feet. The latter will serve her well for swimming, but for now they make her clumsy as a bear cub.

The most striking change is in her coat, once as downy as milkweed and as pale white as the flesh of a birch tree with the bark peeled away. It has now darkened to a soft yellow that reminds me of the switchgrass in the pheasant fields and the aspen leaves that flutter in the trees and carpet the ground in the grouse and woodcock covers we'll hunt in fall.

Belle is not the spastic devil dog that Harper was. She is gentle, nearly to the point of shyness. And attentive—Belle watches Nancy and me more than ever these days. It's as if in just the last few weeks she's noticed a peculiar difference in the two upright members of her pack. She stares so intently sometimes. We purposely ignore her gaze until, overcome by frustration, she'll softly whimper until we stop whatever

Nothing seems to fit. Her tail is too long one day; her head is too big the next. Every appendage keeps losing pace with her thickening legs and hugely padded feet.

29

it is we're doing to look at her. What she's seeking I haven't the foggiest. But once satisfied that she sees it, she toddles off looking for Harper and one of his ears to chew on.

• • •

As tentative as she seems, Belle took to the water without a lick of coercion. But then again, introducing a Labrador retriever to water is a lot like teaching a bird to fly. Once again, in matters of instinct, it's always best that we humans not muck things up by getting too much in the way.

Nancy and I like walking the beach in the evenings. We take both Harper and Belle on those outings, where the dogs run the shoreline unfettered by either leads or commands. When she tires of chasing Harper, Belle likes digging in the slick, wet sand where the waves roll up and fall back, leaving crooked, white, frothy lines like snail trails. Plump as a shoat and happily involved in the business of digging, Belle is not always quick or agile enough to dodge the breaking waves. Lake Michigan has given her more than one soaking over the months, but like a duck she lets the water roll off her back.

We've taken regular forays into some of my favorite covers. There the grouse are drumming. When I find their dust bowls on the wooded two-tracks, I hunker

down until Belle sidles over to give them a smell. She feigns interest, snorkeling in the grit, then bounds off into the bushes, seeking out other smells.

On the two-tracks we cross every mud puddle. Belle quickly graduates to negotiating small streams as deep as her knotty knees. To a little pup that wants to be with you, these obstacles seem no different than a fallen tree across the trail. Belle is compelled by the need to follow.

For her first "official" swim, I choose a shady oxbow on the Platte River that I found in spring while fishing, stalking the grassy riverbanks looking for rising trout. An old beaver dam blocks the lower end, a place I was able to raise a few small browns. Above it, the current runs slack. The water, waist deep, is warm in the sun,

the channel so narrow one could easily toss a stone across it.

I find a place to cross, a gentle slope. Belle has only a moment of uncertainty, a fit of puppy splashing when the sandy river bottom vanishes beneath her feet. Along with words of encouragement, I offer her favorite crud-caked canvas bumper, tossing it into the water in front of her. And with that, the floundering ceases. The retrieve, though not exactly textbook, is cause for grand celebration.

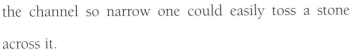

• • •

From sniffing out hidden wings under the corner of the sofa, to finding them in the tall grass in the corner of the yard, the little game I dubbed "find the bird" took on new a dimension this month with the inclusion of the real thing.

The birds I bought from "Pigeon Man" for five dollars each. A hefty sum for such an ordinary bird—that is, until you learn the price includes same-day service and home delivery if he's in the neighborhood. Pigeon Man (himself an odd bird) likes being known as such. Upon our first transaction he even wrote it on a slip of paper—Pigeon Man—along with his pager number.

Apparently, the purveying of pigeons is only a sideline. Pigeon Man owns a couple of dozen highway billboards from here to Grand Rapids. A Lab man himself, he started trapping the birds for his own dogs when the pigeons wouldn't stop crapping all over the scantily clad supermodels in the Calvin Klein underwear ads on the signs.

In his wallet Pigeon Man carries pictures of his "little girls"—two black Labs. Not surprising, both appear identical to the eyes of anyone who doesn't know them. Molly and Sprig. The fact that Pigeon Man's wife took everything in the divorce except for them strikes on his face a sinister smile.

To Pigeon Man I mean no offense, but somehow I'd wager she was as equally comfortable with the deal.

The birds he sold me were great flyers all. Belle again made me seem a masterful trainer. Though I was prepared to let her run amok, to flush the dizzied

pigeons wild and give chase, she stayed closed and quartered the bird field like a big dog.

She ran headlong into the first pigeon and stoned up solid at the scent—head outstretched and tail high, a certifiable point. It's a common occurrence in young flushing dogs upon their first encounter with live birds; the warm feather smell is that overpowering. I imagine the first whiff of a live bird so close is like a blue flash of destiny in their brains, the same thing that has frozen us all at one time or another when the future presents itself like a gift. Yet unlike a human, instead of turning away and not believing the course instinct directs, the dog parted the grass to see what was there.

The pigeon, a black one with a skull-white head, rose on clapping wings, and Belle leapt into the air after it. She chased only a few bounds before stopping short and staring in rapt wonder at the dipsy bird, fluttering lazily away across the great green open, then moving higher against the blue sky. She stood transfixed watching it, as if standing in a light divine.

She stood transfixed watching it,

as if standing in a light divine.

37

JULY

If you have a good hunting dog, then it's likely that you also have a buddy or two like Wayne. Wayne's the kind of friend I rarely hear from unless it's bird season. Not that I hold this against him. Nor do the dogs and I

38

To any young men out there finding

it hard to meet members of the fairer

sex, it is Wayne's advice to get a

yellow Lab puppy.

feel used. He's like a bowling buddy or somebody you play poker with on Saturday nights.

We hunt together because Wayne is good company. Harper has always liked him because he's a good shot, while I am so horribly inconsistent it mystifies. Wayne is safe and courteous in the woods, and he loves dogs even though he's never kept one of his own.

"Dog's are too much maintenance," he says.

For him, anything that hints of responsibility and therefore some semblance of upkeep is something to be avoided. This, of course, includes regular employment, and for our purposes here, the presence of a Mrs. Wayne.

He is one of my few unmarried friends. It never happened, he claims, because he never met anyone who he considered to be the marrying type.

How does this relate to Belle? Well, a good Labrador retriever has many uses. I remember a book entitled *101 Uses for a Lab*. It humorously depicted the Labrador retriever as everything from a garbage disposal to a fishing buddy. Leave it to Wayne to figure out one more use.

When I first saw Belle, my thoughts were of a puppy that would someday grow to rout up rooster pheasants for me, a duck-blind partner that would someday learn to fetch downed mallards after they punched through

the skim ice. Wayne, however, saw a puppy that might help break the ice between him and the legion of women who otherwise wouldn't have anything to do with him.

To any young men out there finding it hard to meet members of the fairer sex, it is Wayne's advice to get a yellow Lab puppy. Or do as he did and finagle a way to baby-sit a friend's dog for the day.

"That little one's a real babe magnet," Wayne said,

never one to mince his words.

But puppies grow up to be dogs, which could explain why I haven't heard from Wayne in weeks. Or could it be that their day at the beach was a resounding success? Wayne may be a bit of a womanizer, but he doesn't kiss and tell. And Belle? She's not upset in the least that he hasn't called. She doesn't act used or jilted at all, even though it'll be the middle of fall before Wayne has any more use for her.

AUGUST

The purple knapweed has bloomed, and now every uncut field, every hillside, is covered with it. The color is soft lavender, like flowers and prom dresses, exactly like the sky just before dark after the sun falls in behind the trees.

One field we go to at dusk looks from a distance as if there is not a break between the earth and sky. A purple plane without a top or bottom—without any depth at all—where the dogs galloping across it look like winged creatures in a dream.

The only problem with this fantasy is the reality that once outdoors, Harper wants nothing to do with Belle.

In fact, it has been made clear to me over the months that my vision of hunting them together will probably have to wait.

Harper doesn't even know the difference between a mere pleasure hike and a hunt. No matter how sparse the cover, in his feeble mind a bird could suddenly bust out at any point and time. Further, I might at that instant whip out from under my T-shirt my trusty side-by-side and blast that crazy cock from the sky.

Harper never has cared much for my Zenlike musings. He doesn't give a whit about sunrises, about the golden sunlight flittering through the trees, the music of the marsh at sunrise, my cosmic insights into our relationship. Or why after he works so hard to find birds that I'm so often remiss in shooting over, under, and too far behind.

At the end of the day, Harper is the kind of partner who's into the body count. Hunting is deadly serious business for him. And I'd wager by how much distance he keeps between himself and Belle in the field that he doesn't want some know-nothing pup nipping along behind him, mucking up his game.

Poor Belle. She is befuddled by Dr. Jekyll turned Mr. Hyde.

I've tried to explain it to her, to warn her that this is what happens when you let instinct override good sense

Poor Belle. She is befuddled by Dr. Jekyll turned Mr. Hyde. . . Outside, she brings Harper gift sticks and particularly interesting pinecones she's found. But he turns his head and runs away like a schoolboy on the playground rebuffing a kiss.

43

and reason. Nancy likes to say that when it comes to hunting, Harper is one burrito short of a combo meal.

This is your brain. This is your brain on birds.

I tell all this to Belle in private. But she only cocks her head and stares. She wags her tail but doesn't understand a word of it. She sees our walks for what they are: a chance to romp and run. Outside, she brings Harper gift sticks and particularly interesting pinecones she's found. But he turns his head and runs away like a schoolboy on the playground rebuffing a kiss.

Against my better judgment I loaded the both of them into the truck and drove to a favorite cover of mine where I knew we'd find a brood or two of grouse.

Strictly a training run, of course. With the season

less than a month away, it was time to give Belle a whiff of the real thing.

The drive to the woods was fraught with an anxiety attack from the big black fella in the back. As we passed through downtown Lake Ann, people stopped and pointed. Given his wailing, the passersby might have thought I was taking Harper to the ovens. Friends witnessing these tantrums all agree that he needs medication. A lot of it. I suppose I've grown used to it. But even for him, this little snit was over the top.

Once we reached the cover, he leapt over the tailgate and busted the first brood of grouse before I had even loaded the blank pistol. Everywhere around me, sticks popped and snapped. The ground trembled and shook. The tops of the little aspen trees shuddered in his wake, a murder of crows took cacophonous wing, then a black flash streaked across the two-track a hundred yards away. Harper. Little Belle saw him, too, and gave chase.

I was running down the road after them, patting every pocket, looking for a whistle that wasn't there, when another grouse went up. And another.

"No! No! No!"

Back across the road behind me ran Harper, with Belle joyously in tow. A big gray grouse split the canopy and veered straight down the road. Six grouse. Then a seventh.

I was running down the road after

them, patting every pocket, looking for

a whistle that wasn't there, when

another grouse went up. And another.

"No! No! No!"

He trounced that cover until there was nothing left. And only then did Harper come back, with Belle absolutely grinning at the fun. For this blatant infraction he showed not a bit of remorse. A vengeful gleam I saw in his eyes.

Harper had flogged that cover, and both he and I knew it. But instead of the thrashing he deserved, I made him run it again. He stayed in perfect range. Belle got birdy once. A pile of deer droppings. False alarm.

At the next cover I left Harper in the kennel. I put Belle down and closed the topper, and that's when the screaming started. A caterwaul as if the death angel was dragging him home by the tail. A quarter-mile from the truck, a half-mile, and I could still hear the screams.

I started thinking crazy thoughts. Begrudgingly I called to Belle and we hurried back along the two-tract to the truck. We rounded the corner, and the screaming stopped. I could plainly see Harper outside his kennel, his nose and tongue clearly visible through the foggy topper glass. Houdini escaped. Inside, the kennel was turned over, the latch on the door busted. I knew better than to let him out of the truck. But no matter; we had returned. And Harper looked rather pleased with himself nonetheless, as if he was certain he had driven the point home: that hunting the two of them together this fall was probably not in the cards.

SEPTEMBER

Surely no tougher gunning exists than what one experiences when woodcock hunting with a Labrador retriever in northern Michigan in September. At this time of year, so grotesquely thick and nearly impenetrable are the places I hunt that I am reminded of the tangles where I used to dog rabbits in my youth. Inside, the covers sport a low ceiling, a leafy overhead canopy that seems woven together as tightly as the fibers in a swatch of wool. So lush and thick that the sunlight can barely get through. Dark and gloomy and otherworldly. The pole-sized aspen, chalky gray, remind me of prison bars.

Yet at the same time the word "enchanting" comes to mind. The ferns under the aspen tops seem magical. They grow to the height of a man's waist and are so dense you literally wade through them in the wake of the dog that's worming around down below.

Should your Lab bump a bird, the window for a shot is small. It exists only in that space between your waist and the back of your head. I say the back of your head because in a northern Michigan woodcock cover you walk bent over. You must, since if you're not crouched low, ducking branches, you'll be swabbing the blood from your lip where one busted you.

47

Nothing you learned at shooting school prepares you for this. So my advice? Forget everything you think you know, and learn to shoot from the hip.

Purists in the pointing-dog crowd may call me a cretin and cringe at the notion of hunting woodcock with a Lab. Unlike a pointing dog that will hold the bird until the hunter casually strolls up, pockets his pipe, and pots the bird on an easy straightaway, a flushing dog doesn't know that moment's hesitation and would just as soon catch the bird himself if he can. The hell with where you are in relation to the goings-on.

With any flushing dog, you need to know that in September you're apt to hear more woodcock twittering away in flight than you see. And you'll almost never be ready should a shot present itself, usually because you're looking down or falling down. And if you do get a shot, it's typically not at the bird itself but along an imaginary arc that you hope the woodcock flew after it catapulted through the belly of the aspen tops.

When you blast blindly into that canopy, green and yellow leaves tumble down like coins glistening in the sunlight—sunlight that suddenly shines blindingly through the newly formed hole. You sometimes shoot a lot, because there are plenty of birds and because Labs are good at finding them. But you will rarely kill a limit in September. So if this be your goal, hook up with a

buddy who owns a nice, steady English setter. That's what I do.

The prospect is not all grim. As in most things, if you persist you will eventually connect. And should this occur, it's certainly at this time you'll be glad you brought your Lab.

Over the years, Harper has returned to me the equivalent of at least one big woodcock dinner—no less than a dozen birds that I did not see fall and would therefore have left to the coyotes.

Still, I contend that people who say Labs are great woodcock and grouse dogs are not hunting in northern Michigan in September. That or they're not eating many birds, which lest we sugarcoat it is why we are out here hunting. Not to mention that it's our duty to knock down a few for the dog once in a while.

The gunning is tough. But with a Lab, it's not an entire wash once you learn a few things. To get a few woodcock for Belle we hunt in the morning, at first light, when the woodcock can often be caught out in the open spots along the edges of the dreadfully thick cover they inhabit throughout the day.

Woodcock don't know the difference between a pointing dog and flushing dog. So they'll usually hold tight no matter what the breeding of the beast breathing down on them. All of which is good and fine for little Belle being that her only experience on birds to date has been with dizzied pigeons and dim-witted preserve pheasants.

Still, when it comes to the tiny woodcock, every flush is a surprise. With such a young puppy, the temptation is to blaze away willy-nilly in the hope of scratching down a bird. Yet you'll find that if you can assuage your killer instinct on the initial rise, get a good eye on the woodcock, and mark it down, you will enjoy a more predictable rise the second time around.

. . . you will rarely kill a limit in September. So if this be your goal, hook up with a buddy who owns a nice, steady English setter.

51

Belle is a little girl. But to tell me

she's making game she utters the most

unladylike sound I've ever heard. It's a

cross between a toilet flushing and a

piglet snuffling under the ferns.

Eventually, you learn to read your Lab as you do the cover. Every dog does something different when bird smell fills the air down there, be it a quickening gait, a head down low and determined, or a maddening herky-jerky slashing of the tail. When Harper is on the trail of a bird, I have seen his eyes roll upward—that great pig-iron head of his reared back, nostrils flaring, mouth slightly agape as if he were a rutting whitetail buck on the trail of a hot doe.

Belle is a little girl. But to tell me she's making game she utters the most unladylike sound I've ever heard. It's a cross between a toilet flushing and a piglet snuffling under the ferns. She delights in smelling woodcock poop, those chalky white splatters that tell us both that the birds are near. Once more, on her first woodcock this September—her first wild bird—she strikes a point. As with the planted pigeon, it's just a flash-point, one she holds only for a second before pouncing.

A clean shot on the rise is out of the question. The bird flutters out like a dust devil of golden leaves twisting upward. It disappears then pops down through the ceiling farther on, settling into the ferns a stone's throw ahead. I take my time, letting Belle work every stitch of cover. We approach from below the bird, giving Belle a quartering breeze, and when she hits the scent her line is direct. The woodcock spirals upward and in a moment of indecision hangs there in the open air, suspended as if trying to determine the proper way to flee. Because I want this one so badly for the dog, the urge to kill this creature verges on the insane. My concentration could be no more focused were I charged with driving the lance through the heart of a winged dragon breathing fire. I don't think about missing. And for once, I don't.

53

At the shot the woodcock seems to pop, a cloud of pearly feathers tumble down in a wash of golden aspen leaves that carried it upward a moment ago. Belle runs to the fall—and keeps running. I watch a tremor in the ferns farther up the hill, then closer, then behind me going away. The temptation is to just walk over there and pick up the woodcock that I know is dead, but I stand firm, giving Belle all the time she needs. After a minute's search and with her no closer to finding the bird, I tell myself that the woodcock must be air-washed . . . that she's just excited and that this, her first, is a big to-do. I whistle her back. "Dead bird. Dead bird." Belle, all snorts and grunts, spins circles in the area of the fall but comes up empty and moves on.

... the light is dim yellow, the color of

warm butter. I let her lick and snuffle

the woodcock until it resembles a

crumpled, wet washcloth...

Finally, the tension breaks me. I get down on hands and knees and see the woodcock just as my little piggy finds it (finally) herself. But I stave off the notion to pick it up myself. However unlikely, this woodcock is her very first wild bird. I sit there under the ferns watching her at last snuffle it up. Belle licks the woodcock. "Fetch it up," I say, at which she saunters over, chomping merrily. And for a while we sit down there, disappeared under the ferns where the light is dim yellow, the color of warm butter. I let her lick and snuffle the woodcock until it resembles a crumpled, wet washcloth, all the while stroking the little furrow between her eyes, running my fingers over the back of her pointy little melon head. Then I look around, and all at once the view down there is marvelous. The stalks of the ferns are like mighty tree trunks, columns spaced apart, nearly blocking out the sun. We are very small. This is what I think. And for the first time I can see everything ahead of us, and everything behind.

F A L L

THE GOOD OF THE GAME

Woodcock, grouse, pheasant, or duck. Choose any fowl that you hunt and that a dog might bring you. Bury your face in its breast feathers, and even then you only have an inkling what the bird must smell like to the dog. The odor is so strong, even to our pitiful olfactory sense, that to the dog it must be as powerful as that whiff of leafy, mossy dampness that hits every hunter right smack dab in the face every October. Yes, bird hunting has its smells, but how about its sounds?

It's said by those who are musically inclined that every sound has its own distinct color. Duck hunters who've heard the whistler's wings and the mallards calling across the backwater during a fiery sunrise shouldn't find this hard to believe. Or better yet the pheasant hunter, for no one can deny that when a rooster pheasant goes up—with the raucous cackling and all that wild color—it's like a skyrocket on the Fourth of July.

We know the smells and sounds and colors of bird hunting. Surely the taste is a dry one, like cottonmouth, with the bitter hint of adrenaline in the back of the throat. And the feeling? Well, when you're behind a Lab, it is anticipation.

It's a burning in the legs when the dog's tail gets to spinning and you're caught lagging behind. It's that sudden, cold rush when the bird goes up and you're slightly off balance and not exactly sure where you want to be.

And it's the feeling of oneness you have with the dog—with everything—when she finally roots that bird out from whatever god-awful tangle of brush it has wormed its way into and when, after the shot, she brings it, at last, to hand.

OCTOBER

If the dogs and I ran country where pheasants and wood ducks lived in ample numbers, I think we would hunt only these gaudy birds in October.

I grew up chasing pheasants behind my father's dim-witted farm hounds back when Pennsylvania still had a huntable population of wild roosters. Wood ducks I stalked alone on a dead stream that ran through the dark hollow behind our defunct farm. There, under autumn leaves the color of fire and sun, I found them feeding among the oaks or lounging on the deepwater pools at midday. A drake woodie in full plumage is so gorgeous that I feel a strange kind of punch-drunk love for them. I am always mesmerized by the feathers of a wood duck, agog at the comic-book colors, the almost garish beauty of the bird.

Alas, northern Michigan is big-timber country, a land where there are no real pheasants (they live down south along with a modest number of genuine bobwhite quail, both of which I long one day to see). As for the wood ducks, although some nest here throughout the summer, the first frost—the first puff of cold autumn air—sends them packing long before the dawn on opening day.

A drake woodie in full plumage is so gorgeous that I feel a strange kind of punch-drunk love for them. I am always mesmerized by the feathers of a wood duck, agog at the comic-book colors, the almost garish beauty of the bird.

59

This is not to suggest that my new home doesn't have plenty of birds for the dogs and me to love. Michigan is fly-over country for any winged creature struck by the inclination to trek to warmer climes once the weather turns cold. October marks the beginning of "the flights." Depending on what circles you run in, this can refer to either the start of the woodcock migration or the first flocks of puddle ducks and divers that begin trickling down into this country from the north.

And did I mention the grouse, the only gamebird tough enough to winter here?

My passion for hunting wild birds, both waterfowl and upland, is rivaled only by my desire eat them and render a *glace de gibier* from their bones. Again, it's but one reason why I've grown so fond of Labrador retrievers: No matter what I decide to hunt on a particular day, the dogs merrily accommodate me. Always willing to oblige my whimsical nature, they never care about the bird or the cover as long as a retrieve is included somewhere in the program.

This year, however, Belle has forced me to straighten up and prioritize. She's proving to be a good woodcock finder. Contrary to dismal mutterings of other hunters decrying "a downturn in the cycle," we've bumbled up oodles of them in the covers we hunt. And since my goal is to build Belle's confidence her first season, we stick with those things she's proving good at.

The same winds ridden south by the migrating woodcock blow bare the trees and make the shooting a tad easier every day. Even so, I'm sorry to report I've missed far more than I'd like. In the case of the woodcock, my urge to knock down these birds for the dog remains far out of proportion to both the size and demeanor of such a timid, all-accommodating creature.

In these woods, grouse are the only bird for which such wrath becomes an asset. That's because you don't hunt grouse so much as you suffer for them. Unfortunately, having at this time only experience with woodcock, which sit tight and are patient with the dog's noisy, frantic effort to sniff them out, Belle is downright stupified by grouse.

When she hits a hot patch of scent, the odor is so mesmerizing that she will refuse to move from the spot where the bird obviously stood. While the grouse hotfoots it somewhere up ahead, Belle snuffles the spot, utterly floored that the source of the heavenly smell isn't hiding right there under the aspen leaves. Grouse don't suffer long such amateurish antics. Inevitably, I hear

them blasting out in front leaving us sucking backdraft.

After a month, the woodcock in certain covers are predictable as to their whereabouts. With the flights on, we see new birds almost every day in the same old covers. A hillside that yields only six flushes one day will the next yield a dozen. And what's uncanny is that the newcomers almost always occupy the same places, which allows for little end-around maneuvers that have helped in getting Belle those all-important retrieves.

The same old grouse toy with us seemingly every day. They've eluded us for so long I've taken to naming them: Old Lester, Crazy Grouse, and Colombo (he always has us figured out). Together, we managed to bushwhack one I had nicknamed El Grouso, which had duped us no less than a dozen times before, always winging off the top of the same little knob while we were dinking around looking for him at the bottom.

Every day we hunted El Grouso, I heard him bust off that same hilltop and once caught a glimpse of him gliding over the little beaver pond toward the cedar swamp on the other side. I let him get by us in this way for weeks, then yesterday did a little flanking maneuver—walking along the edge of the pond myself while Belle dinked around the confounding web of scent he left for her in the aspens down in the valley.

The trap was set.

I heard the flush then saw him winging toward me through the treetops. El Grouso banked hard to the right, into the trailing edge of a load of number 6s I placed there for him. He tumbled into the cattails at the water's edge, and Belle, hearing the shot, sped down the hillside herself, locating the big gray bird in a pile.

Not the most graceful find. She half slid, half flopped onto the grouse—the way Pete Rose used to steal second base. But what a bird! I let Belle prance around with him for a while, huffing and snorting like a fat lady laughing.

I think she liked it. Yes. She liked it just fine.

She half slid, half flopped onto the grouse—the way Pete Rose used to steal second base. But what a bird! I let Belle prance around with him for a while, huffing and snorting like a fat lady laughing.

NOVEMBER

I'm not some purist who thinks you have to have decoys and duck calls for hunting to qualify as waterfowl hunting. As long as it's legal and fair, I'm as big an opportunist when it comes to shooting ducks as my dogs are about retrieving them. No deep-seated hang-ups about jump shooting or float hunting here. In

Whereas Harper hates to be talked to while he's hunting. . . Belle actually seems to enjoy the chatter and the occasional pat on the head.

fact, as winter sets in and the north wind bears down, a hard freeze blankets every lake, swamp, and beaver pond for two hundred miles in every direction, leaving the rivers as the only open water. Ice. All that frozen water everywhere and the calendar showing almost a whole month left in the duck season.

With her calm and quiet demeanor, Belle is shaping up to be a perfect partner, whether in the blind or the boat. Simply put, she's not as spastic as The Harps. She sits calmly and without protest. Whereas Harper hates to be talked to while he's hunting (he barely tolerates any of that touchy-feely stuff, either), Belle actually seems to enjoy the chatter and the occasional pat on the head. Affection in the field merely throws Harper off his game.

• • •

Most of duck hunting is work, albeit the best kind. Like training a hunting dog, you only get out of it what you put into it. But it's work all the same. There are usually decoys to be set and decoy bags to be wrestled with, blinds that need dressing, and—in my case—a canoe that requires a strong back if any forward momentum is my goal. But such burdens carry light for the duck hunter.

On this morning, however, Belle and I have only the cold to contend with—that, the snow, and a hoarfrost

on the windows inside the pickup so thick it takes an ice scraper to shave it off.

The defroster in the Toyota's on the fritz again.

Belle takes her place on the passenger-side floorboard, her chin resting on the edge of the seat. The snow around the boat launch shows that we are the first to put in today. The current churns over rocks in midstream, swirling in tiny whirlpools that glimmer in the moonlight.

While I heave the canoe down from the truck, Belle runs along the bank looking for god-knows-what. Then she's out into the water, paddling toward the middle.

"Get outta there, you crazy!" I holler.

This is becoming a little routine of hers, every morning, before shoving off. Only this time when she hops into the boat and shakes, the water is so cold it feels like a hundred pinpricks stabbing my skin.

• • •

There are really only two kinds of waterfowlers in this world: those who hunt with retrievers and those who don't. Dog men are typically staunch blind hunters, solid ground being far and away a better launching pad than a tippy old canoe for a lumbering water dog. Out here on the river—at this time of year—the cold keeps most everyone else away, except maybe the wandering farm kid prowling the banks, looking for a mallard to pot.

So Belle and I shove off knowing there's not another place to put in or take out for the next ten miles, knowing, too, that there's probably no one ahead of us. Nothing but cedar swamps and snow and the possibility of ducks around every bend.

The float will be two, maybe three hours long. I asked Nancy to meet us around noon, down by the tracks and the stone bridge where the county road goes over.

When I start paddling, the eastern sky's the color of a pumpkin's insides. Sweepers, those windblown and

beaver-chewed cedar and aspen trees that have fallen over in the water, make paddling tricky the first hundred yards. And the rocks. You always have to keep an eye out for the rocks. But the current winds out before long; the river runs deeper, slower, and I guide the canoe in tight to shore.

Belle lies between my feet, craning her head to see over the bow. I trust her already to remain steady, and if need be a paddle to her backside serves as a not-so-subtle reminder to sit still. Two heavy shells in the side-by-side, the gun resting on the gunwale at arm's reach. Everything ready for the first chance.

We round the first bend. I am half-expecting to see a brace of mallards (two drakes, please) but instead spy a deer on the snowy bank. A doe, she lets us drift down on her without moving, confident in her camouflage, I suppose. Her hide's as gray as ash. But with the snow, she's lit up like a billboard and doesn't seem to know it. Belle never spots her, and quite frankly that's fine by me. Watching the deer out of the corner of my eye, I steer the canoe so close I can see her frost-covered whiskers. We drift past without her so much as twitching an ear.

The next bend is coming up, so I dig the paddle in deep and start into the turn, glancing back toward the deer, only to find she is gone.

• • •

It's cold down here in the river valley, even with the sun now over the trees. This is hunting, I think, the way it should be. I'm a stalker, not a stand hunter at heart. Not that I don't appreciate a few good mornings spent in the duck blind. Still there's the nagging notion: If you're sitting on your can it ain't huntin'. It's something my father might say.

We hear the ducks before ever seeing them. Belle springs into a crouch and I hiss at her, "Down." Twenty yards ahead, four mallards rise up from the river on white waterspouts. Two drakes in the rear, but all are away before I can even get the gun to my shoulder, disappeared over the treetops.

Gone.

• • •

When float hunting, it helps if you know the river, if you know from experience the slipslops and cutbanks where the ducks like to lounge and feed. My experience comes from trapping beaver here in the spring. Even so, the ducks always take me by surprise. And without a shooter in the bow, I find myself hoping for a stupid duck—or a bunch of stupid ducks, like this small group of mallards that plays a game of leapfrog with us for the next quarter-mile.

It's only after flushing them a half-dozen times without a shot that the canoe gains their confidence and we again drift within twenty yards. Still, the shot I manage is a poor one. But it's enough to tumble one of the drakes into the tangled mess of brush on the river's edge.

Again I swap the gun for a paddle, digging backward hard into the current to bring us in to shore. Belle leaps onto the bank, snow up to her chin. I follow the ensuing chase by the sounds of twigs popping, wings flapping. Belle appears then on the bank upstream, the mallard catching a ride. Its colors shine, its green head iridescent. And the drake's orange legs kick dead air when I rest it belly up on the floor of the canoe.

Our next bit of luck comes at an oxbow, or what will become an oxbow in the next hundred years or so. It's one of the places where Belle learned to swim months before, a place that's fed by a trickle of current on the north end. Enough of a current that there's always a patch of open water.

Without the dog, managing a shot here alone would

. . .without a shooter in the bow, I find myself hoping for a stupid duck. . .

71

be next to impossible from the canoe. So what I do it this: With Belle at heel, we wade through the thigh-deep snow, circling the "pond" until we're positioned upwind. I listen for a moment. Nothing. Then I let Belle noodle around until she bounds through the wall of brush and I hear ducks—the murmur of mallards and then a rush, a waterfall sound of wings pulling for the sky.

So many ducks come over that I have a hard time picking just one. The first shot creases the air in the center of them. But as I bear down on the second, the duck I want flips sideways and back and spirals down, making a hollow *thud!* when it hits the ice on the other side.

The pond is mirrorlike, unblemished save for an old fracture—a white line, like a healed-over scar, running its length. Willow trees line the far bank, their branches brushing against the ice in the breeze. I step out onto it, to assure myself that the dog is safe, then kneel down ready to receive her bird.

Back at the boat and another drake mallard in the bow. I lean heavily on the paddle, pushing out into the current again. The next bend is coming up fast. I eye the gun and the dog, then hunker down and guide us into the turn.

WINTER

ALL DOGS DIVINE

Inside every Labrador pulses the heart of a lion. It's their spirit we adore—the essence—that befitting mix of grace, dignity, and a touch of whimsy, so genuine, pure, and unfettered it can seem almost otherworldly at times.

It's hard not to think of all dogs as divine, each an angel sent down to brighten our lives. You see it most clearly in winter, when everything is bleak, barren, and drab, when the trees are looming shadows, bark as gray as cemetery stone, when the wind outside's like the whisper of a ghost.

A yellow Lab racing over the empty, snow-covered landscape can chase away winter's air of awful finality like a beam of sunlight burning away the fog.

With his golden partner, the hunter walks into winter's dusky maw and instead of gloom finds the land heavenlike, alive and aglow with possibility. Perhaps it's in the way the dog dodges and darts, creasing the snow and turning on a dime. But on days like this, when everything seems tired, asleep—nearly dead and dismal gray—a good dog can honestly make you feel as if there's a bird, the promise of hope, over every rise.

DECEMBER

When it comes to having multiple dogs, there are two schools of thought: The first says that you can never have enough, the second that, like wives, you can only do justice to one at a time.

I've drifted between tents in both camps over the months. I like having more than one dog. For one thing, in spite of the utter indifference Harper often shows Belle, I believe dogs prefer the company of their own kind. The only problem, if there is one, comes with those pangs of guilt I feel when taking Belle hunting and leaving the big fella at home.

Harper was downright miffed the first time Belle and I slipped away together. Alone during those wee morning hours and with nothing to do but brood about it, he did a thorough job of chewing to toothpicks the wooden legs of a dining-room chair. Destruction of property is totally out of character for Harper, and he hasn't done anything like it since, though trying to get out of the house without him remains a chore.

Since it's not every day I smack the alarm at 4 AM and leave the house with a gun, there's never any real chance of fooling him as to the day's intentions or into thinking Belle and I are doing anything other than going hunting. Still, I try, going so far as loading everything

Harper was downright miffed the first time Belle and I slipped away together. Alone during those wee morning hours and with nothing to do but brood about it, he did a thorough job of chewing to toothpicks the wooden legs of a dining-room chair.

into the truck the night before. It's the culmination of many amateurish methods of deception.

Belle has a slight edge on the number of days afield. Something I'm reminded of every time I back out of the drive and see the headlights pan across the big window in the living room, where Harper sits pouting, his best *How-could-you-man?* face pressed against the glass.

Yet there are no more birds to show for it. Regardless of which dog has had privilege, our hunting has been decidedly unremarkable. The woodcock are long since gone, ridden a wind south to warmer climes. Grouse have been spotty all season, which is enough of a reason to leave the survivors alone this winter. The birds we did find in December all flushed from trees. Midday or the middle of the afternoon, it didn't matter. They were up in the aspen branches feeding on buds. We found them in trees so consistently that I started looking for the grouse as if they were squirrels. So we left them alone in favor of the ducks. The ice that is apparently keeping the grouse from their snow burrows has also conspired against us, confining the hounds and me to hunting the river south of town. There the mallards and black ducks that pass by every morning have proved wary of my tortured wailings on the call.

December's only surprise comes on the last day of the duck season, a morning so bitterly cold that were it

not for the dog I would gladly stay swaddled in bed under the down comforter, spooning my lovely wife.

Out of the truck, Belle runs gaily ahead on the well-worn snow path we've trodden in our daily forays. In the half-light, the stars above glistening, Belle is a dark shadow loping over the snowfield to that predetermined point, an alder-choked bend in the river where I pitch out a half-dozen decoys then hunker down on the shoreline and begin our frozen vigil.

It is a long time before we hear teams of mallards murmuring *tuka-tuka-tuka*. Every morning they pass overhead in staggered Vs, and every day I wonder where they are headed. There is not a cornfield standing any more, not a patch of open water save for the river, which offers a place to lounge but, I imagine, little in the way of food. I've asked Belle what she thinks, but she has been no help at all. Aside from a swishing tail cutting a wedge in the snow, she sits quietly staring skyward, pondering, always hopeful, the embodiment of faith and belief that perhaps this is the day one of the ducks will peel away and commit to our modest little setup bobbing in the river's flow.

Everything puppy-looking about her is nearly gone, except for the eyes (do the eyes of a Labrador ever look old?) and a few roly-poly folds of puppy blubber clinging to her haunches. But she's still easily distracted by anything airborne, prone to breaking down the bank after tumbling leaves and black-capped chickadees.

This is the last day. Hunting season, the impetus for having a dog in the first place, is almost kaput. But I feel no remorse when the morning passes without a shot fired. We have had a good season. Better than I could have hoped.

Once the sun is over the hill behind us, illuminating the snowbanks with a pink glow, I collect the decoys without a second thought that something wonderful has occurred over the months: During this period, Belle has grown into a gun dog, though as I shoulder the bag and

. . .something wonderful has occurred over the months: During this period, Belle has grown into a gun dog, though as I shoulder the bag and crawl out of the river, I can't for the life of me pinpoint the exact moment when it happened.

. . .she prances circles about me,

holding the duck in a full-body wiggle,

her tail slapping my shins in applause.

crawl out of the river, I can't for the life of me pinpoint the exact moment when it happened.

I whistle up Belle, who is off exploring upstream. We march back across the field, that huge swath of snow, my yellow dog and I not wearing one stitch of white when a lone mallard appears off in the distant sky. At first, it is a speck on the horizon, something that I mistake for a crow. Now, inexplicably, it strafes the field, the white underbellies of its wings flashing like a strobe, and passes low over Belle, who gets a good eyeful and despite my pleas to the contrary gives merry chase.

Belle is prone to chronic fits of deafness, another pesky puppy trait or, more likely, one of the many oversights in my training regimen. Once at the river the drake banks into the wind, making a wide arc over the cedars. Coming back around, passing nearly beyond range, the duck looks back toward the dog, seemingly more concerned with Belle than the open end of my scattergun.

I shoot . . . and shoot again.

Two utterly breathtaking misses.

But then, when it is little more than a fluttering fleck over the river, the duck falters and drops from the sky as if cut loose from a string suspending it. I try to imagine the scene from Belle's perspective: It must have seemed magic, the bird falling from the heavens purely

as a result of her resolve to chase it down. I can see that air of cockiness in her stride. And in her look. The dog comes hurtling back across the snow, her ears flapping, the wing of that mallard like a veil, draped coyly over one eye. Then she prances circles about me, holding the duck in a full-body wiggle, her tail slapping my shins in applause.

JANUARY

The snow falls, and it keeps falling. And the north wind blows. At nighttime, in bed half asleep, I lie listening to the trees outside bend and creak. Limbs occasionally snap under the weight of the snow that's piling on, and the dogs stay up late listening, too, staring at the shadow fingers waving on the windowpane, exchanging random barks and low, deep-throated growls. Belle, a light sleeper long free from nights spent in the kennel, is usually the instigator of this guttural canine dialog. Everything that bumps the roof or scratches the walls is a potential intruder threatening her pack.

And then come the nights I wake from a dream to find her staring at me, nose to nose, sucking my wind like a cat. Just staring. I must have been either talking in my sleep or jerking around in the middle of "the falling dream." But when I open my eyes, she's right there, the tip of her tail wagging. Then my nose gets a lick, and she quietly lies down again to resume the watch.

Chalk this up to a budding motherly instinct. Belle will be a year old January 20. Sixty pounds and built like a fire hydrant. She's grown to be a chunky little blond, half a hand shorter than Harper's twenty-seven inches at the shoulder. This month, Harper began to take a seemingly incestuous interest in his buxom little sister.

For a week it seems the days Nancy and I have dreaded are finally upon us. Never mind the frequent visits to the vet's office, the hundreds of dollars spent every year on dog food, dog toys, and dog-related gear. You will truly realize how far you've fallen, how deep you've sunk into dogdom, and how you'd do damn near anything for your dog when you're standing in the line at the pet store about to lay down cash money for a pair of doggie diapers. You realize in that instant that, indeed, you've become one of "those people"—a certified dog nut.

We long considered the complications of Belle's first heat given that Harper, her housemate, is a fully intact male. A biddable albeit slightly antisocial canine, Harper has never shown much of an interest in others of his kind, female or otherwise. In fact, the sudden attention he began doling out to Belle early this month served as an indication that love might be in the air.

Harper's an inexperienced lover so the advances he's

You will truly realize how far you've fallen,

how deep you've sunk into dogdom, and how

you'd do damn near anything for your dog

when you're standing in the line at the pet

store about to lay down cash money for a

pair of doggie diapers.

85

Harper's an inexperienced lover so the advances he's making now lack savior faire. To show he's smitten, Harper simply runs around with his nose firmly ensconced in Belle's keister.

making now lack *savior faire*. To show he's smitten, Harper simply runs around with his nose firmly ensconced in Belle's keister. Or when roughhousing in the living room, he jockeys for position only to get rebuffed with a hip fake and bite on the snout. He tries another tack at wooing: licking Belle's ears until they hang down sodden, like a couple of wet dishrags. For the most part, she seems to enjoy this new attention, even if she appears naïve as to what motivates it.

Though physically capable, Belle is far too young to make puppies, a fact Nancy and I are well aware of. So for a time I remain vigilant against the hanky-panky getting too far out of hand. Then on the day we begin packing Harper's bag for a stint in the kennel, he returns to a state of indifference. Only a couple of days later, the ribaldry starts again. Then stops.

Strange, however, that if presented with his favorite racket ball or chew toy for throwing, Harper is easily distracted from his bent. Once again, having his head so much in fetching proves a boon.

You often hear of retrievers that would rather fetch than eat. Harper is a certified member of this pathetic lot. I know because at mealtime I've tested him. But this comes as no surprise given his lineage. A story I heard of his father, Webshire's Honest Abe, serves to best illustrate the point.

Vern Weber, who owned the titled field champion until the dog's death, often studded Abe for what amounts to monthly mortgage payment for most. Abe's blood was hot for retrieving, a trait he obviously passed on as evidenced by the number of his progeny that went on to amateur, open, and national field-trial titles.

It's customary that canine coupling occur at the home of the stud. Vern told me of one such tryst where after shutting Abe and the willing bitch in the garage, Vern and the female's owner retired to the kitchen and a cup of coffee. Since this was the other gent's first time, a bit of awkward chatter ensued. The bitch was in "standing heat," so the entire breeding business wasn't to take more than couple of minutes. So after a few moments of jibber-jabber Vern and the other man decided to check on the lovebirds—only to find poor, misguided Abe sitting pretty in the middle of the floor, staring not at the lovely ebony mistress offering herself to him but upward, transfixed by the hypnotic swing of a tennis ball hanging from a string. Vern used the hanging ball as gauge when pulling his vehicle in and out of the garage and had forgotten to take it down.

Our plan is to breed Harper and Belle, but not quite yet. After a season spent hunting with her, I am convinced that the pair will someday throw a wonderful, capable litter of puppies that, if destiny shines, will be right down the middle between the parents when it comes to their birdiness, drive, and desire.

We've consulted our veterinarian and found that once past her first heat, Belle can be put on "doggie birth control" (what will they think of next?). But for now the game is wait and see. Belle seems to be sending all of us confusing signals, which I told Harper just to get used to, as such is typical of a female.

FEBRUARY

February is a hard month. Hard on all in our house: men, women, and dogs. When I think of winter in the north woods, I think of the hardness of ax handles and pine knots, the dull thud of firewood bumped together to knock off loose snow. I think of the slick shine of black ice on country roads and the white ice on every lake and pond, ice so hard and thick people drive their snowmobiles and trucks across it instead of walking through the cutting wind to their ice shanties. Winter is still here. Winter is long and nasty. But bellyaching about it does no good.

Up here, February is a good month if you enjoy things like ice fishing and skiing. On days when the snow isn't too crusty and there's nobody else out on the ice, Nancy and I take the dogs along when doing both.

When I think of winter in the north woods,

I think of the hardness of ax handles and

pine knots, the dull thud of firewood

bumped together to knock off loose snow.

89

February is good, too, if you enjoy how clean the cold can make you feel. At night, we often don snowshoes—always when there's a full moon, a moon big and orange rising in the east, a moon that looks like a fire in the sky before peeking out above the trees. The stars gleam white and yellow. The air is so clear, so cold, you can see their different colors. It's a cold you can taste going down.

February is good if you like wood fires, if you like the scratch of wool against your skin, if you like the smell of cinnamon and orange peels simmering in the cast-iron pot on the woodstove. But it's not good—not good for anybody—if you think too hard about spring, which in February is such a long, long way off.

• • •

To add to the feeling of "cooped-uppedness," Belle went into full-blown heat the first week of the month. The real deal this time, it was a special time in our house. Still, the first couple weeks were easy. Keeping the dogs apart was simply a matter of my taking Belle into my tiny, cramped closet space of an office and closing the door. She slept beside my chair (exactly as she is doing now as I write these words) while Harper snoozed outside the door.

But soon that would no longer do, as far as he was concerned. No longer do tennis balls and rubber dummies dissuade Harper from what nature is commanding. And he has become the wolf outside my office, sniffing, scratching, and whining. Belle sits inside watching the door, occasionally alternating her glance between me and the hubbub outside. We make occasional breaks for the door downstairs so that she can tend to her business. Every day the tussles get more and more comic. Harper, realizing he doesn't

91

have much time to sow his wild oats, dispenses with all pleasantries and tries jumping on board and getting in a few good licks before Big Daddy Ogre Man (that would be me) hollers and busts up the party. Belle, looking at him with her best "come hither" look is no help. Finally, it's time for Harper to go. So I make a hasty appointment for a week's stint at the kennel, and that, as they say, is that. The house is quiet once again.

• • •

February is a time for remembering things. And I have a lot to remember from the past year. This is a month for reflection, for sizing up how we spent our days, and it seems a good time to sit down and ponder

if Belle has, in fact, become another dog of my dreams. And she has, leading me to where I started—to wondering how I am so lucky that I should have two dogs under my charge, two great dogs that have chosen to partner with me.

I'm partly convinced that dogs grow to become exactly what we ask of them. Sometimes it just happens. Usually it doesn't have much to do with words or actions. It is, I think, beyond us somehow. Dogs are a mirror of the stuff we have inside, and however unwillingly, we end up creating them in our own image, with both the bad and the good that we often keep out of sight, the kinds of things very few people have the stomach to admit or the eyes to recognize. Dogs, however, see it all. Every not-so-good dog I've ever met has embodied, in one form another, all the not-so-good traits of its owner. Likewise my own dogs—especially Harper—who is at times impetuous, bullish, and a clod. Belle is at times both shy and manipulative. She has become everything that Harper is not and therefore everything that I could have hoped for.

February is a time for walking. Belle and I head out to the same fields we trod over during summer, though nothing looks the same covered by snow. We walk along the river and through the same woods we hunted in the fall. Though the woodcock are long gone, the grouse are

It seems a good time to sit down and ponder if Belle has, in fact, become another dog of my dreams. And she has.

still here. Belle bumps one from its perch atop a white pine, and we both watch it going away through the tree-tops and swirling clouds of powder snow.

February can make a person melancholy, and I suppose I was in one of those moods—Nancy calls them "funks"—when we were heading home the other day. The memory is as clear and crisp as the late-winter air.

Consumed by banal thoughts, it occurs to me while walking, watching Belle fully grown, running over the snowy white, how short her life will be, a life as fleeting and delicate as the air she now huffs, those tiny white vapor clouds that trail behind her and so quickly dissipate. Our life together, when measured in the grand scheme of things, will last just as long . . . a brief instant.

Each of us has grown a little older over the year. Each of us has learned much. I look at the trail we cut through the snow heading home. Her tracks are no longer a puppy's but a dog's—they might be the tracks of any dog—and my prints, with my snowshoes on, look foreign to me. It is all right there, as if written on the land. I look ahead at the field, the barren white, then back the way we have come, and find those tracks already blown over, disappeared by the wind and snow.